Praise for *Dreaming of Glistening Pomelos*

"Flo Oy Wong does not simply write poetry. With her talent for expertly blending words and analogy, Wong transports readers through time and space to a place in her personal history that resonates deeply no matter one's ethnic background. Wong's poetry evokes a whole body experience that leaves the reader changed and charges us to contemplate the lives and dreams of both yesterday's and today's immigrants and their families with deeper understanding. *Dreaming of Glistening Pomelos* is unequivocally a superb collection of poems."

— Kaecey McCormick, Cupertino Poet Laureate, Cupertino, CA (2018-2020)

Creative conviction courses through her,
resurrects luggage dragged home from
concentration camp after WWII,
transforms rice sacks into canvases,
immigrant lives writ large. Now

her poetry explores past and present,
speaks to beauty, pain, reverence.
Her creative conviction endows her
the courage to endure critiques,
risk exposure, then reap rewards.

— Ann Muto, former Cupertino Poet Laureate, author of *Open Passage*

Flo Oy Wong's poems flow like wooden fish songs that immerse us in the rhythm, language, and customs of her native Toisanese Gim Sahn culture. The old vanishing, if not forgotten Gold Mountain village colloquial vernacular and immigrant sensibility is vividly recalled in Flo's fresh and direct narrative voice, which captures simple and ordinary human vignettes of her working-class childhood in a family-owned Chinatown restaurant in the post-World War II era of Oakland, California. Flo's poetry sings with poignant sensitivity and loving reverence for the first generation of long-suffering pioneer Chinese immigrants responsible for shaping our Chinese American history and identity.

Wong asks the question,
Tell me, Muse,
How do I begin the saga of the Gee clan
that lived in a small village
blessed by the Dragon God?

This collection richly answers how.

— Genny Lim, SFJazz Poet Laureate, author of *Paper Angels*, co-author of *Island: Poetry and History of Chinese Immigrants on Angel Island, 1910-1940*

Dreaming *of* Glistening Pomelos

Poems & Drawings by
Flo Oy Wong

Pomelos, native to South and Southeast Asia, are citrus fruit that resembles large grapefruits. During the Lunar New Year, a traditional Chinese home would display pomelos along with pyramids of oranges and tangerines. Pomelos are both sweet and bitter; the bitterness is found in the enveloping membranes around the segments. These parts are considered inedible and are usually thrown away.

© 2018 *Dreaming of Glistening Pomelos* by Flo Oy Wong.
All rights reserved.

ISBN #: 978-1-7326198-0-7

Printed in the United States of America

Illustrations by Flo Oy Wong

Author photo and photographs of all illustrations by Edward K. Wong, except for the images of "Wiping the Table" and "Phoenix, Me," which were photographed by Curtis Fukuda

Book design by Margaret Copeland, *terragrafix.com*

Ordering Information:
This book can be ordered from all major online booksellers.

*For Benjamin Wong Halperin,
Sasha Wong Halperin,
and Peter Edward Wong*

Contents

List of Illustrations ix
Preface xi
Poet's Statement xiii

What Will Climb into My Heart? 3
The Color of Despair 4
Among Ancestral Bones 5
I Lean on a Song. I Follow the Story 6
As the Wind Murmurs 7
Under a Moonlit Sky 8
In Search Of. 10
Tell Me, Muse: My Older Sister Speaks 12
A *Gim Sahn Hauck* 15
Gell Ngnoy Yee: Call Me Auntie 18
Back When Heaven Was Just a Whisper 19
House of Fiery Daughters 21
My *Baba*'s Voice Walking through the Rooms 23
Icee Clem 24
Ai Joong Wah, Great China 27
Between Her Mother and Father 29
In the Sun-Painted Afternoon 30
Savoring the Moment 31
Building Mansions 32
This Immigrant Woman, My Mama 36
At the End of Her Day 37
Mama, If I Lived on a Star 39
My Mama's Lament 42

From That Moment On 43

I Was That Man You Saw 45

Like a Ghost. 46

Fragments of My Childhood 47

A Paper Napkin 48

Flying Like Confetti. 50

In the Busy Kitchen 51

Within the First Order. 54

Lincoln School. 55

We, the Outside Kids 56

The Spoon Man 57

Being Delivered 58

Som See Nai 60

On My Wedding Day 62

Acknowledgments. 63

Afterword 65

About the Poet 67

List of Illustrations

Oakland Chinatown Series
Graphic Pencil Drawings
Collection of Artist, unless otherwise noted

Cutting the Birthday Cake, 1986 . . . . front cover

In the Back Booth, 1980s[*] 2

In Chinatown, 1983 20

Mom, Pop, Me, 1984 22

On the Table, 1984 25

Great China: The Front Counter, 1985[***] 26

Standing on Webster Street, 1983[*] 28

Soaring Above Chinatown, 1988[****] 34

Phoenix Me, 1980s[**/****] 41

Enriched Rice, 1989 44

In the Kitchen, 1984[***] 53

Wiping the Table, 1984,[*/**/***/****] (Collection of Felicia Joy Wong and Jon Halperin) . . . 59

---

[*] Previously published in *Sweet and Sour: Life in Chinese Family Restaurants* (Yin & Yang Press, 2011)

[**] Previously published in *Contemporary Citizenship: Art, and Visual Culture: Making and Being Made* (New York: Routledge, 2018)

[***] Previously published in *The Making of an Artist: Desire, Courage, and Commitment* (Bristol: Intellect, 2018)

[****] Previously published in *70/30: Seventy Years of Living, Thirty Years of Art* (San Francisco: Asian Pacific Islander Cultural Center, 2013)

Preface

With sensitivity, thought, and grace, poet and visual artist Flo Oy Wong uses words and images to create positive energy and connections among all people. While text has been long a key component of Wong's visual work, her poems now return the favor with words that evoke her keenly attuned sense of the visual world.

In her richly layered mixed-media art, ranging from intimate objects to monumental installations, Wong frequently enmeshes fragments of hand-painted, embroidered, and beaded text within her visual imagery. She also embellishes the text imprinted on materials such as rice sacks to highlight the personal, familial, and cultural symbolism of the fabrics and other substances laden with meaning with which she assiduously fabricates her work. The seeds of many of her poems can be found in the hand-stitched narrative that recounts her husband Ed Wong's youth in Augusta, Georgia, in *Baby Jack Rice Story* (1993-1996); in the carefully collaged textural recounting of her mother's immigration experience in the series of suitcases that comprises *My Mother's Baggage* (1996-1998), which reveal the secrets of Chinese immigrants who came to the United States; and in the painstakingly beaded phrases that speak to the traumatic experience of imprisonment of nuclear scientist Wen Ho Lee in *Kindred Spirit* (2001-2003).

Literary scholar and critic Amy Ling[1] writes, "For women of Chinese ancestry, writing is not solely an act of self-assertion but an act of defiance against the weight of historical and societal injunctions." It is no small thing for Flo Oy Wong to give voice in these poems to her own experiences, to family secrets, and to the trauma, resilience, and hopes she sees in the world. In these poems, Wong's defiance of the silencing she experienced as a woman of Chinese descent is both gentle and persistent. With determination and deep respect, even reverence, she honors her own memories and those of her family, her husband's family, and the Chinese immigrant community. The ordinary becomes extraordinary in Wong's reflections on everyday life. Her deeply felt connections with her surroundings and the people and other beings that populate her world infuse her visual art and her poetry alike.

From her narratives composed of fragmentary memories buried and exposed over time, to urgent testimonials that bear witness to experiences weighted by histories of marginalization and silence, Wong's poetry is richly layered and evocative. These poems are deeply personal, sometimes provocative, giving voice to stories often hidden and untold. On the occasion of her eightieth birthday, Wong offers these poems as her gift to the rest of us.

— MELANIE HERZOG
Dean of the School of Arts and Sciences
Professor of Art History
Edgewood College
Madison, Wisconsin

---

[1] Amy Ling, *Between Worlds: Women Writers of Chinese Ancestry* (New York: Pergamon Press, 1990)

Poet's Statement

At the age of nine, I heard poetry.
At the age of eighteen, I attended the University of California, Berkeley.
At the age of twenty-two, I graduated from the University of California, Berkeley.
At the age of twenty-two, I became an elementary schoolteacher.
At the age of twenty-three, I was married.
At the ages of twenty-eight and thirty, I gave birth to my children.
At the age of forty, I became a visual artist.
At the age of seventy-five, I started to study poetry in earnest.
At the age of seventy-seven, I was diagnosed with chronic pain.
At the age of eighty, I am publishing my first poetry book.

From the age of nine, I have been fascinated by poetry. Now that I am turning eighty, I give myself this gift, a book of art and poetry titled *Dreaming of Glistening Pomelos,* which is filled with memories of my childhood in Oakland, California's Chinatown. I honor my immigrant parents, Gee Seow Hong and Gee Suey Ting; our family; and the workers of our family's restaurant, *Ai Joong Wah,* Great China. I share the little-known travails of my Mama and *Baba,* who worked from sunup to sundown to feed the Chinatown and other local communities during the 1940s to early 1960s.

While writing my poems, I studied the works of Ted Kooser, who won the 2005 Pulitzer Prize for poetry and was appointed in 2004 the United States Poet Laureate. I was also enchanted by the writings of Li-Young Lee, winner of the American Book Award in 1995. In my local community, I became active in the vibrant poetry environment created by the Cupertino Poet Laureate program, studying with former laureates Amanda Williamsen, Ann Muto, and the present laureate, Kaecey McCormick. I am a member of the Cupertino Poetry Circle, led by Ron Miller. Our monthly gatherings at the Northwest YMCA are times of poetic sharing, enjoyment, and community. Other inspirational writers — my sister Nellie Wong, and Erica Goss, and Keiko O'Leary gave illuminating workshops, which I attended in order to hone my skill.

I would not have been able to put this book together without Kaiser Permanente's Pain Management Rehabilitation Program (PMRP) in Santa Clara, California, co-founded by Barbara K. Gawehn and Karen Peters. While organizing the book, I practiced deep breathing through the entire process. I worked in thirty-minute segments, religiously taking breaks from the computer. I implemented multiple tools such as meditation, Feldenkrais, qigong, and yoga stretching that allowed me to manage my pain as I worked.

I worry at this time about the anti-immigrant stance of our country's leaders. I stand with all immigrants. In 1933, my mother became an illegal immigrant because of the 1882 Chinese Exclusion Act. The statute prohibited wives of Chinese laborers from coming to the U.S. with their husbands. Still, my mother entered this country illegally as my father's sister. Because of my parents' courage, I am able to be a viable American who creates works of art. As a woman artist and poet of color, it is essential that I tell my stories from an insider's point of view. Now, I am a thriving elder who contributes to the American table of art and culture.

Dreaming *of* Glistening Pomelos

What Will Climb into My Heart?

What will climb into my heart?
Will it be the time *Baba* brought
Mama, his second wife, to America
As his sister and not his wife?
Or the time that Mama called me
Her *lucky daughter*[*] because she said
I brought her beloved son to her?
Or the time my developmentally challenged sister,
The oldest in our family,
Patted her pregnant stomach, saying
In our spoken dialect, Hoisan-wa,
"*Hoo bebe*, carry baby?"
Or the time my second sister persuaded
Mama to let me to join
The Brownies at Lincoln School,
Such an American thing to do?
Or the time my third sister and her future husband
Took me to the Emeryville baseball stadium
To see Casey Stengel and the Oakland Oaks?
Or the time my fourth sister wrapped
My future husband's graduation gift to resemble
A black-gowned graduate in cap and gown?
Or the time my fifth sister walked down
The church nave as my matron of honor,
The purplish color of her dress
Matching the stained-glass window?
Or the time my younger brother,
Our only boy in the family,
Sketched the most beautiful horses I had ever seen?
There is enough space in my heart for all.

---

[*] In my family and other Chinese families in Oakland Chinatown, a girl who preceded the birth of a boy was called the lucky daughter.

The Color of Despair

We never know what memory will do,
How sometimes it dazzles as ascending sun,
How sometimes it radiates in rice fields,
Where water soaks ancestral feet.
Or how memory can be found in a darkened corner
Of a decades-old brick house where
A carbon ring speaks of meager meals cooked long ago.
A few rice grains bedded below stringy greens,
A scrawny chicken foot dipped in soy.
Of burlap coat threaded with sweat
Our ancestral peasants wore in low-yielding fields.
They toiled,
Scratching livelihood one day to the next,
Bending, pulling, bending, pulling.
Memory swells, sometimes recedes
To harsh scrapes born of howling existence,
Hope evaporating in driving monsoon.
Torrential rain slashes, slashes, slashes.
Or how memory can be found in a hoe,
Hacking ground into shriveled worms,
Vegetables' roots dry as dust.
Ancestors light incense
Their lives the color of despair.

Among Ancestral Bones

On this first day of the Year of the Rooster,
Clouds part to reveal flowery cherry blossoms
In homes, temples, and businesses.
Brooms are forbidden to sweep today,
Because good fortune must be confined to homes.
To sweeten his annual reports of families and workers
in Heaven,
We smear the Kitchen God's lip with honey.
Mounds of oranges, sweetmeats, watermelon seeds, and candy
Flavor dreams of hardworking ancestors,
Whose calloused hands still stiff from the plow
Are perfumed for this day of flowering.
Children beat drums, cymbals clang,
To wake the prancing dragon,
Whose dance unwinds and swirls,
Among ancestral bones.

I.
I Lean on a Song. I Follow the Story*

As the wind whispers
In *Baba*'s village,
The banyan tree
Casts its shadow.
Listening,
I lean on the song
I follow the story
Of the time when *Baba*,
A young boy then,
Switched the cow,
Harvested rice grains,
And kissed his mama
In his slender night dreams
When the moon flickered
In the midnight sky,
To reveal shimmering stars
Shining on *Baba*'s village below,
Where a trail of smoke marked
My ancestors' adobe abode.
Although I have never seen *Yeh Yeh*** or *Nai Nai*,***
Never heard them call my Chinese name, Ling Oy,
In raspy voices,
Never stroked their weathered faces,
Nor tickled their scrawny bodies,
I dream of them now.

---

* Li-Young Lee, "Build by Flying," in *Book of My Nights* (Rochester, NY: BOA Editions, Ltd., 2001)

** *Yeh Yeh* is Cantonese thlee yip (fourth dialect) for paternal grandfather.

*** *Nai Nai* is Cantonese thlee yip (fourth dialect) for paternal grandmother.

II.
As the Wind Murmurs

As the wind murmurs
In *Baba*'s village,
The banyan tree
Casts its lingering shadow.
Attentive,
I squat in the crisp shade to listen
With my *Gim Sahn** heart
Borne from AMERICA, my homeland.
Long-ago *Baba*, a young boy then,
Resided in this hidden village.
He raced to school on these paths,
His book bag pounding his body.
In the one-room school house,
He intoned droning sounds
Of the teacher's low-pitched words,
Which *Baba* learned by rote.
Outside of school,
He switched the cow,
Harvested rice grains,
Washed threadlike greens in the muddy pond.
In his slender night dreams
He kissed his mama and his *Baba*.
As the creamy moon glowed
In the midnight sky,
Shimmering stars lit *Baba*'s village below,
Where a wispy trail of smoke
Coming from the makeshift chimney
Marked my ancestors' adobe abode.
Although I have never seen them,
Baba's parents, whom I would call
Yeh Yeh** and *Nai Nai*,***
Never heard them say my Chinese name
Ling Oy, Beloved Daughter,
I come now to forage for their spirits
And that of my sweet *Baba*.

---

* *Gim Sahn* is the Cantonese thlee yip (fourth dialect) for Gold Mountain, the U.S.
** *Yeh Yeh* is Cantonese thlee yip (fourth dialect) for paternal grandfather.
*** *Nai Nai* is Cantonese thlee yip (fourth dialect) for paternal grandmother.

Under a Moonlit Sky

I.

My siblings and I travel to China
For a visit to our ancestral village, Goon Du Haung,
Where our three older sisters were born.
Arriving in the small hamlet, I see for the first time
The pond in front of crumbling adobe houses,
The water buffalo immersed in the cool water,
Swishing its tail languidly while residents stare at us.
We are guests from *Gim Sahn*, America,
Come with candy and fruit for everyone.
Standing in the stifling heat, I hear giggling
Of three young girls with bowl-shaped haircuts.
They smile, then look shyly at their rubber-tread sandals.
I think of my China-born sisters, now well along in their years.
What were they like?
Did they skip under the banyan tree?
Chase one another,
Kicking up dirt at their heels?
Swat mosquitoes buzzing around their heads?
I imagine my second oldest sister as a youthful child chanting

II.

Holding hands under a moonlit sky,
I feel the softness of your flesh.
We dance towards the banyan tree,
Open like a leaky umbrella.
Shards of moonlight beam upon us,
Offspring of gods and goddesses.
Our village, Happy Dragon,
Is filled with rice paddies.
We smell cow dung,

Newly defecated on arid soil,
Taste bits of rice straw
Caught between our teeth,
Hear crickets,
Chirping arias of flight,
We swing our arms,
As if we have ascending wings,
Glide by the Field God's shrine,
Dreaming of glistening pomelos.*

---

* Pomelos, native to South and Southeast Asia, are citrus fruit that resembles large grapefruits. During the Lunar New Year, a traditional Chinese home would display pomelos along with pyramids of oranges and tangerines. Pomelos are both sweet and bitter; the bitterness is found in the enveloping membranes around the segments. These parts are considered inedible and are usually thrown away.

In Search Of

Let me go in search of . . .
The concrete gray of Harrison Street,
The cracked sidewalk squares,
Divided by lines,
So different from *Baba*'s paths of childhood,
Seeded under the banyan tree,
Where ancestors gathered long ago.

Let me go in search of . . .
Dreams of *Baba*'s immigrant heart,
Fetishes for abundant growth buried in fields,
Where ancestral breasts and torsos
Were seared by blistering sun,
Where flimsy rice stalks were grazed
By scrawny worms.

Let me go in search of . . .
His untied queue,
A knotted one,
Is a symbol of oppression,
Coiled like a snake around
Baba's sun-hardened neck,
His young life hidden by great walls
Of struggles,
Where his parents' toil once folded
Into dense manzanita bushes.

Let me go in search of . . .
His son who will swallow the moon,
Daughters who will knit links to earth
Across a powerful ocean,
Lashing moistened shores,

Where their footprints will mark
A new land, a new home.

My poem is inspired by a line in Jason Shinder's poem "Tuttle Crossing, Ohio" in *Stupid Hope: Poems* (St. Paul, MN: Graywolf Press, 2009)

Tell Me, Muse: My Older Sister Speaks

Tell me, Muse,
How do I begin the saga of the Gee clan
that lived in a small village
blessed by the Dragon God?
There is a shrine in the field,
Oh Muse, where the Protector
looks out on rice paddies,
where bronzed peasants
work from sunup to sundown.
The women wrap their heads in scarves
billowing in the wind.
The men's pants are rolled to their knees,
feet soaked in muddied rice fields.
The sun beams on these workers.
Oh Muse, their muscles are strong,
but their hands are cottony soft
as they harvest rice grains.

Along the creek there are water snakes.
A man jumps in the creek and twists
a snake by the neck.
"Soup!" he shouts.
"Dinner tonight," another says, smiling.
Oh, Muse, these peasants are hard workers.
In the dark of the morning,
they splash their faces with cold water,
because the fire from the *kang**
is not fully billowing.
After eating cold rice,
chopsticks clanking their rice bowls,
they drink lukewarm tea,

then move slowly out to unyielding fields.
Oh Muse, this is a small clan,
living behind overlapping manzanita bushes,
which mask their presence.
If Mama did not lead the way,
I would have been lost.

My Mama,
She is a part of this clan, this field.
She married my *Baba* after his first wife died,
leaving behind a baby daughter.
After Mama wed *Baba*,
he returned to the Land of the Flowery Flag,
America, to earn money where streets
were supposedly paved with gold.

Oh Muse, there is no gold
here in our homeland,
only dusty fields, buzzing insects,
streams that are sometimes full.
There are hidden weeds,
insects that might bite our feet
at any moment.
Oh Muse, the field's name is Happy Dragon,
but I don't think people
like Mama are happy here.
Sometimes her groan thunders,
as if her voice is erupting
from the center of the earth.

Oh Muse, my *Baba* is not here.
He returned to America,
Land of the Flowery Flag,
where the streets are definitely

not paved with gold.
To get there, oh Muse, villagers,
mostly males of different ages,
cramped like sardines in oily cans,
sail across the *Ai Ping Yeung*,
the Pacific Ocean, that leads
to lives unknown.

Oh Muse, I do not want
to leave my *Poo Poo*, grandmother.
Let me stay.
I am a *gwai slueoon neuy*,
A good granddaughter.
I will wade into paddies,
bai sin, light incense sticks
to pray to ancestors,
stuff rice straw in the *kang*,
drape vegetables in the torrid sun,
sweep the earthen floor,
shoo rats away.

---

* A *kang* is a brick platform built across one side or the end of a room warmed by a fire beneath and used for cooking and sleeping.

A *Gim Sahn Hauck*

Mama — My Mother

I look at the man my Mama chose,
My husband-to-be whom I have never seen.
Dressed in a dark suit, shiny black shoes,
He is a *Gim Sahn Hauck*[*] who toiled for years,
Far-flung across the sea from our homeland.
Now that he needs to wed again,
He comes to Ai Leong, our village,
Because his Mama picked me.
I will marry him . . . become his second wife.
Oh, he is nervous,
Sweat beads on his forehead.
He is handsome, but I did not choose him.
His right eye is smaller than the left,
His body odor is different from
The dung-perfumed men who toil in our fields.
When I marry him I will live in *Gim Sahn*,[**]
Away from my Mama,
Whose wispy hair grows white and thin,
Whose bones are flooded with aches,
Who gives me scarce meat,
While chewing meager greens.
When I marry . . . my belly will be filled.
I will collect cow dung no more.
Pluck rice stalks no more,
Stuff rice straw in the smoking *kang*[***] no more.

Baba — My Father

I look at the woman my Mama chose,
My wife-to-be
From the neighboring village of Ai Leong.
I did not choose this woman.
Can she . . . give me a son?
I need a son to carry my surname, Gee,
To the next generation.
Will she care for my first child, a daughter,
Whose mother has passed?
Will she bring me comfort,
Caress my heart?
In the sultry heat of this day,
She dares not look at me for long.
I see her three-corner eyes, *thlom gauck ngon*,****
Small nose, drooping shoulders, calloused hands,
Large feet hidden in embroidered slippers.
Will she be still in my arms,
Tender to my touch?
In *Gim Sahn*, our life there
Will be arduous, our days — long.

Poo Poo — My Mother's Mother

I look at the handsome man I chose
For my winsome, raven-haired daughter
Who at the age of twenty-one,
Still collects cow dung near our adobe home
In land the weary Field God abandoned.
Ngnoy guh leong neuy, my beautiful daughter,
I found a *Gim Sahn Hauck* for you.
I have lived my life in this desolate land.
Now, you will live yours in faraway *Gim Sahn*,
Where I hear that their streets are paved with gold.

You will
Collect cow dung no more,
Wet your feet no more,
Pluck rice stalks no more,
Stuff rice straw no more.
Feast now . . .
On your last grains of rice
With me.

---

* *Gim Sahn Hauck* is Cantonese thlee yip (fourth dialect) for Gold Mountain guest.

** *Gim Sahn* is Cantonese thlee yip (fourth dialect) for the name early Chinese immigrants gave to the United States of America.

*** *Kang* is a platform built across one side of a room warmed by a fire beneath and used for cooking and sleeping.

**** *Thlom gauck ngon* is Cantonese thlee yip (fourth dialect) which literally means an eye with three corners, usually an eye with single lids.

GELL NGNOY YEE: CALL ME AUNTIE

On Angel Island near the open road,
A distance from *Ai Fow*, San Francisco,
The ocean billows.
I think of you, my *Gim Sahn** husband.
Our daughters and I have traveled
A long way to be with you.
We are latched behind barbed wire,
Soldiers with guns here.
Second daughter . . . shivers.
She asks . . . what she has done wrong.
What do I tell her?
I worry . . .
Will we answer the questions correctly?
In *Fah Kee Gwok*,** America, I am your sister,
Not your wife.
"Shhh!"
I warn our daughters,
"*Maw Gong, Maw Gong*,
Don't tell, don't tell.
Secret.
Maw hom ngnoy doo Mama.
Do not call me Mother.
Gell ngnoy yee,
Call me Auntie."

In November 1933, my mother, a "paper sister," was detained at the Angel Island Immigration Station along with my three older sisters. They stayed for six days for interrogation purposes before leaving to join our father in Oakland, California.

* *Gim Sahn*, Gold Mountain, in Cantonese thlee yip (fourth dialect), is another Chinese name for the United States of America.

** *Fah Kee Gwok* in Cantonese thlee yip (fourth dialect) means Land of the Flowery Flag, one of several Chinese names for the United States of America.

BACK WHEN HEAVEN WAS JUST A WHISPER

Back when Heaven was just a whisper,
When my immigrant family was growing,
Back when my parents thirsted for chromosomal seeds
To birth their wanted son, I was born,
Back when autumnal winds wrapped the land,
I cried keen sounds, bundled in startling cloth of rainbow hues,
Crimson signifying good fortune.
Life beckoned and I answered,
Dancing with waving arms, slender piano fingers,
Catching my breath in diaphanous webs of sisters.
I swooned in the hand-me-down crib.
Inhaling my sisters' love, I was soft and harsh.
Back when my parents still desperately wanted their son,
My tendrils started to spread and I tapped the sun's energy,
To eventually beam between shimmering moon and stars.

This poem is influenced by poet Rita Dove.

HOUSE OF FIERY DAUGHTERS

When silence is louder than thunderous drums of the Lunar New Year,
a time when prancing dragons joyously spit out green lettuce symbolic of money,
when firecrackers explode the heart of Webster Street, I run after the festive
cacophony, remembering *Baba*'s and Mama's long-ago ancestral homeland,
a place where rice stalks swayed in monsoon-flooded fields. Howling winds
swept into *Baba*'s ancient abode that could no longer house them. After coming
to our new country, my *Baba* and Mama resided in a house of fiery daughters,
until they birthed a son.

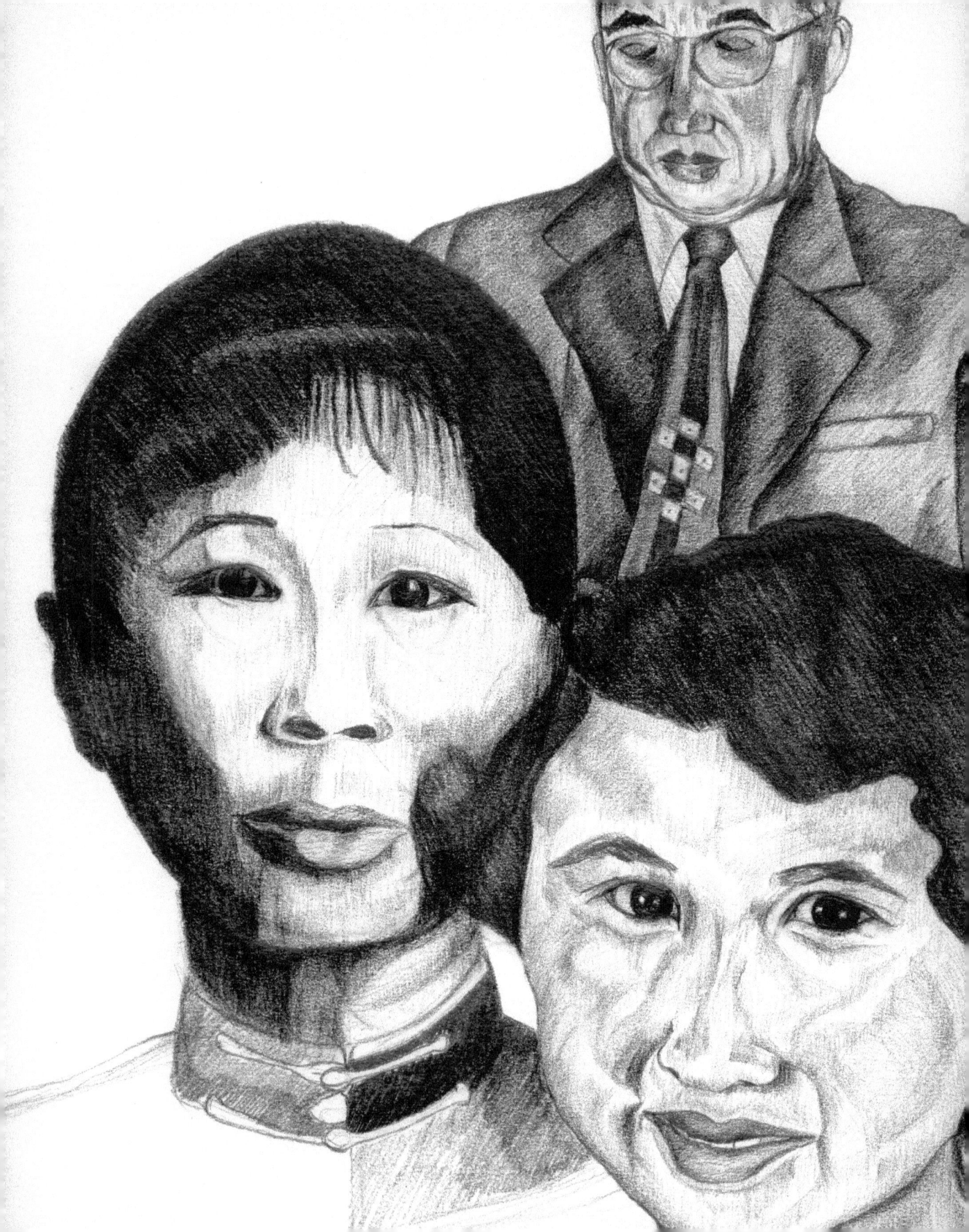

My *Baba*'s Voice Walking through the Rooms

My *Baba*'s voice, walking through the rooms
Of our yellowed Victorian house on Harrison Street
In Oakland, California, during the 1940s,
Clings to the musty lace curtains filtering light into our lives.
I, his sixth daughter, go near the flecked windows of our immigrant life,
Sniffing odors of the torn bark in *Baba*'s impoverished village,
In China known as Goon Du Haung.*
I see my paternal grandmother,
A dimming candle on a splintered shelf,
In a faraway adobe house with sooty floors.
Her parental wisdom extends across the sea,
Where, later, my *Baba* keenly imparted our family's values,
Teaching my siblings and me the gift of giving,
And the gift of accepting.
In *Fah Kee Gwok*, America.
Whenever his China-born spirit was thirsty or hungry,
I, his sixth daughter, listened to his homeland stories,
Especially when he talked about the beautiful rolling hills
Resembling the back of an undulating dragon
Rising above his humble village.
Now, he is long departed,
But, still, *Baba*'s voice nurtures me
In the folds of my fermented life in America.

---

* Goon Du Haung was the name of our ancestral village in China until Communist rule. Goon Du Haung is now known as Loong On, Happy Dragon, because the nearby hills resemble the back of a dragon.

My poem is inspired by a line from Li-Young Lee's poem "Black Petal," in *Book of My Nights* (Rochester, NY: BOA Editions, Ltd., 2001).

Icee Clem

Dressed in his overalls and scuffed shoes,
Baba reaches for my hand.
I am wearing a hand-me-down dress and shoes.
I smile, holding *Baba*'s hand,
Wondering where we are going.
We walk towards Eighth Street where
There are grocery stores, fish markets, and more restaurants.
Food odors mix with the mustiness of shoppers.
At Eighth and Franklin Hamburger Joe's reigns.
Juicy hamburgers and chunky French fries,
Dream food of Chinatown children.
Waiting for cars to stop, we cross
With nary a word between us.
Passing the reddish-brick apartment complex,
Housing African Americans of all ages,
We continue towards Broadway,
Where on one side of the street Bank of America
And other businesses are located.
On the other side, there is a jewelry store and a movie theater,
Which sells ice cream of many flavors to passersby
Through a window open to the street.
"Ice cream, *Baba*," I say.
We walk to the jewelry store's opened window,
"*Icee clem*," he says.
The jeweler gestures toward the movie theater.
"There."
At the theater's window, *Baba* repeats, "*Icee clem*."

Ai Joong Wah, Great China

Ai Joong Wah!
Great China!
Tanh Gawnh!
Restaurant!
Ook Loon Haw Ngin Fow!
Oakland Chinatown!
Ghee Geong* *Bok*!
Ghee Geong *Sim*!
Uncle Ghee Geong!
Auntie Ghee Geong!
Hoy goong lah!
Start work now!
Gah feh!
Coffee!
Min bow doy!
Parker House rolls!

Ping Gwah Pie!
Apple Pie!
Bow woon hoon!
Wrap won ton!
Kee hoy!
Wait on tables!
Mought hoy!
Wipe the tables!
Slai pawn wawn!
Wipe the dishes!
Slai gah feh woo!
Wash the coffee urn!
Hoy goong lah!
Start work now!
Hoy goong lah!
Start work now!

This poem is written in Cantonese thlee yip (fourth dialect).

* *Ghee Geong* is my father's name in Cantonese thlee yip (fourth dialect).

This poem was previously published in *Contemporary Citizenship, Art, and Visual Culture: Making and Being Made* (New York: Routledge, 2018).

Between Her Mother and Father

The child walks between her mother and father, gripping their hands. Her father's hand is a bit more sandpapery than her mother's soft touch. His hands are reflective of the years that he worked as a shipyard welder during World War II. The child looks around, checking to see if her six siblings are nearby, but they aren't, so she skips and jumps gleefully. The three of them, in a rare moment together, swing their arms and walk to the corner, passing dusty storefronts, some flecked with dead flies.

At the corner they turn left, immediately hearing the buzz of the Filipino barber's clippers. The customers are quiet, a contrast to the rushing traffic hurtling along Eighth Street. The child moves ahead with her parents, smelling the reeking odor of chickens about to be plucked at the lively poultry store. The street is busy with customers at the grocery stores, picking up bunches of *gai lan, bok choy, yeurn sai*,* ingredients for a tasty home-cooked meal. It is in this moment that the child's mother unexpectedly smiles at her sixth daughter while picking a winter melon for their family dinner.

---

* *Gai lan, bok choy, yeurn sai* are Cantonese (third dialect) for Chinese greens.

In the Sun-Painted Afternoon

In the sun-painted afternoon,
I, the youngest girl of six sisters,
crouch in the arid backyard
behind our Chinatown restaurant,
strewn with rotting wood.
My fingers itchy, I wanted to pick
the dark leafy greens known as *gow ghee*,*
my favorite Chinese vegetables for soup
I wished Mama would cook every day.
I could hardly wait to strip the leaves off the stems.
Keong Sook,** the cook who had planted the *gow ghee*,
worried that I would pull the vegetables out too soon.
So, he put up a cardboard sign written in Chinese ideograms,
*"ngnan hon sow but doong,"*** eyes see, hands don't touch.
On this summer day, *Keong Sook* saw me running
through the kitchen, heading to the backyard.
He chased after me.
"Keong Sook," I squeaked in a hopefully contrite voice
When he saw me stooping by the *gow ghee*.
He glared, his knuckles pressing hard
Onto the sides of his smock.
I said no more and retreated, a footstep at a time,
my itchy fingers in my pockets.
Some other time, I thought, when he isn't at work
then I would touch the *gow ghee*.

---

* *Gow ghee* are dark leafy green vegetables used for Chinese soups. When picking them only the leaves were taken. The stems were left in the ground to grow new leaves.

** *Keong Sook* — At our family's restaurant we called the workers by their first names and usually added *sook*, an honorary title for uncle. *Keong* means strong.

*** *Ngnan hon sow but doong* is Cantonese som yup (third dialect).

Savoring the Moment

Baba walks quietly into the upstairs bedroom in the back of our house, carrying a freshly made roast beef sandwich from our Chinatown restaurant. It is eleven in the morning. The lunch crowd hasn't filled the restaurant yet, so he has come home to check on me. I am ailing. I smile a sleepy grin and say "*Baba,*" although "Pop" is at the tip of my tongue. My siblings and I always call him "Pop." He hands me the wrapped sandwich and sits by my side. "*Heck san woo je,* eat your sandwich," he urges. Biting into the delicious sandwich, I chew the Kilpatrick's bread slathered with mayonnaise and stuffed with thin slices of rare roast beef. I munch slowly, savoring the moment. When *Baba* sees that I am eating well, he gets up to leave. I choke a bit, wanting this sandwich moment to linger. Outside, *Baba* gets into his car. I watch him through the slats of the open Venetian blinds, clutching my half-eaten sandwich. *Baba* drives off. It is time to feed hungry customers.

BUILDING MANSIONS

You didn't live a vacuous life, *Baba*,
Not when you weighed prime-rib roasts, pork loin, veal
On a scale that hung behind the large restaurant kitchen.
Not when you sat in the tiny office with the open window,
Focusing on the wooden abacus to calculate
Food and supply expenditures.
Not when you brushed flowing ideograms,
Showing the cost of running the restaurant.
Not when you worked behind the Formica counter,
Making urns of coffee, its odor permeating our pores,
While you dreamt of building mansions for your six daughters
And a son.
You taught us that life is a two-way street,
And that knowledge and education are pathways to a
Substantive future for those of us (especially your six daughters),
Who are nonwhites in this country.
Not when you cherished Mama who stayed behind in our village,
By sending money to hire a tutor you made sure
That she, an illiterate village woman, could learn to read.
With the money you sent Mama also was able
To purchase a daughter of an impoverished family,
Who became our family's servant, a *moy nuey*.*
Some years later, after settling in with you in Oakland, California,
Mama chased the assailant who nearly shot you to death.
When Great China Restaurant opened in 1943, she
Flipped golden-brown pancakes, stirred beef stew,
Which hungry customers would soon consume.
Your days were arduous, too, *Baba*.
Running the restaurant six days a week.
You relaxed at home — cooking for yourself late at night,
Gardening in the front and backyards (I can still see the calla lilies)
And drinking glass after glass of *Ng Gah Pei*,**

Whiskey of Chinese immigrant men.
You drank
To irrigate your compassionate heart.

---

* *Moy nuey* is Cantonese thlee yip (fourth dialect) for a servant girl. This girl was sold to our family. She stayed with Mama and my three older sisters in our ancestral village. When it was time for Mama to come to the U.S. in 1933 she found a suitable man to marry her servant girl.

** *Ng Gah Pei* is the liquor that *Baba* and other immigrant men drank in Oakland Chinatown. The Ng Gah Pei, bottled in Hong Kong, came in a bulbous brown bottle engraved in English. A label in Chinese identified the contents. The alcohol content was 96 proof.

This Immigrant Woman, My Mama

After the stockpot has stopped gurgling,
with pieces of bones swirling
among tendrils of celery
and bits of green onions,
after slices of beef kissed with ginger
have been stir-fried to juicy crimson
and before slumber visits
on yet another work-filled day,
Mama rests nude on her bed,
her supple body the color of ivory.
While standing on wooden pallets
to ladle pancake batter on the grill,
she never stood still.
She lies quietly at home now,
her achy body sinking near the edge of the bed,
her back exposed, strands of alabaster hair,
with sprinkles of gray radiating a greasy odor.
I stare, watching her body lift and fall.
I like to see this up-and-down rhythm,
a respite from fatigue tethered
to working twelve to thirteen hours a day at
Ai Joong Wah,* our family's restaurant.
Sitting on the bed next to her,
I place a steamy towel on her back
to cover taut muscles, after which I rub in Bengay.
It is in this quiet moment we sculpt our lives together,
this immigrant woman, my Mama, and I.
My hands and fingers knead repose . . . gently,
hoping to erase the weight of weariness
because she and *Baba* dared to dream
of a better life for their children.

---

* Ai Joong Wah is Cantonese thlee yip (fourth dialect) for Great China.
This poem is inspired by Li-Young Lee's poem, "Early in the Morning" in *Rose* (Rochester, NY: BOA Editions, Ltd., 1993).

At the End of Her Day

Mama yawned at 5:00 a.m. when she turned over in her bed.
Releasing a sour taste in her mouth as she stretched,
Catching a glimpse of her family's village in China in her fading dream.
She looked for *Baba*'s imprint on the bed.
The crinkly part of the sheets he had slept on was empty.
ZZZZZZZZ — the sound of his shaver.
A sign that she and *Baba* would soon be riding their green
Chrysler sedan to the bosom of Oakland Chinatown
On Webster Street between Seventh and Eighth.
Mama unlocked the glass door of Ai Joong Wah,* our family restaurant.
Her rhythm differed from *Baba*'s when the restaurant opened,
Because she was the fry cook who made breakfast —
The best golden-brown pancakes, scrambled eggs, tasty omelettes, and French toast,
For hungry customers lined up at the door by 6:30 a.m.
Baba settled in the tiny office to check the printed menu,
To clack the wooden abacus, to count coins and dollar bills for the cash register.
Soon the other cooks, waiters, and dishwasher arrived.
Still Mama seldom took a break. Too much to do.
Wearing her blue uniform which sloped over her stooped shoulders,
She waited on customers during lunchtime, carrying plates with freshly made food,
To those who sat at the salmon-colored lunch counter and the few wooden booths.
Many of the customers were men who lived at the Salvation Army a block away,
Or Oakland policemen, shipyard and factory workers, and others.
The hectic restaurant day did not allow my beautiful Mama time to care for herself,
No moment to check her lipstick or to fluff her grease-soaked hair.
She worked all day until the night sky leaned into navy blue evenings.
It was then she finally took off her splattered apron
And sighed, a signal terminating her lengthy workday.
She allowed herself to smile, quietly contemplating
What she would soon be watching on the black-and-white television set.

Her third daughter and son-in-law were the first family members to own an
    RCA television,
So, at the end of her day in the late 1940s, Mama would soon watch
The Lone Ranger, Hopalong Cassidy, and Gene Autry gallop into her evening.

---

* Ai Joong Wah, Great China Restaurant, was the name of our family restaurant in Oakland Chinatown. We ran it from 1943 to 1961.

A previous version of this poem was published in the Autumn 2016 issue of *Blue Collar Review*.

Mama, If I Lived on a Star

Mama, if I lived on a star,
I would flash celestial energy,
Shoot bolts of love to you,
Surround you with sweet words
I denied you when you were alive,
Because bitterness clouded my heart.
I would plant swaying bamboo
In the forest of your life,
So that when the wind blew
You would love me and your other *jook sing** daughters,
Whom you said tethered you to suffering,
For the reason that we were born female.
But, then you wisely, with your peasant wisdom,
Told me that I have *haw meng suey*,** good karma,
I do, Mama. My life is rich.
To balance the many banquets of hardship
You lived through,
I would serve you platters of sweetmeats.
When you came to this country,
You could not be who you were born to be,
Assuming a false identity that *Baba* bought.
You came as a "paper sister,"****
Later, you had to marry, in name only, another man
To make your American-born children legal Americans,
Because the U.S. immigration law
Prohibited Chinese men, like my *Baba*, from bringing
Wives to this new land that did not
Want Chinese to settle here.
When I was one-and-a-half years old,
A relative nearly fatally shot *Baba*,
Blood splattering the living room curtain,
In our Victorian home on Harrison Street,

In Oakland Chinatown.
You courageously chased the shooter,
Onto the streets,
Not worried that he still had his weapon.
You bolted from our house,
My sisters, Nellie and Leslie, following you,
Your apron loosely tied over your housedress,
Brocaded slippers barely supporting your hasty steps.
You screeched, "*Gew meng ah, gew meng ah,*"****
Loosely interpreted — save his life, save his life,
meaning your husband who lay bleeding
on the living room floor.
Two men heard you.
They tackled the fleeing assailant,
Held him until the police came.
Mama, come live on the star with me now.

---

* *Jook sing* is the node in between segments of a bamboo stalk. It is a metaphor to describe American-born children of Chinese descent born in a foreign land.

** *Haw meng suey* is Cantonese thlee yip for good karma. It can be interpreted as the flow of a good life.

*** Paper sister is a term, like "paper people," for women who entered the U.S. under false identities from 1910 to 1940. In order for my mother to enter the U.S., she assumed the identity of my father's sister when she was, in truth, his wife.

**** *Gew meng ah* in Cantonese thlee yip (fourth dialect) is literally translated as save a life.

My Mama's Lament

AI . . . . YA!
Ghee . . . . slin foo ah!
Ah Bing Fook ah uh Baba wah!
Gew . . . . meng ah!
Gew . . . . meng ah!

OH . . . . NO!
WHAT . . . . suffering!
Bing Fook shot *Baba*!
Save . . . . him!
Save . . . . him!

"My Mama's Lament" is a reimagined bilingual poem written in Cantonese thlee yip (fourth dialect). In April of 1940, a village cousin shot my father in a business dispute at our home in Oakland, California's Chinatown. Following the shooting, my mother chased the assailant as he ran from our house. She shouted something like these reimagined words. Two men heard her. They assisted in the capture of the shooter, who eventually was jailed. My father survived. In 1986, I started a new visual work, "Eye of the Rice: Yu Mai Gee Fon," a rice-sack art piece which addresses my father's shooting. It is now in the collection of the San Jose Museum of Quilt and Textiles in San Jose, California.

From That Moment On

In childhood, I lived in a rented house,
With thick doors as if to keep the enemy at bay.
There was a grand staircase that I,
Head covered with a thin green blanket,
Walked down, pretending I was a bride.
Long ago, my *Baba* lay wounded
On the living room floor,
Injured by a distant relative.
Three bullets had pierced *Baba*'s body,
Another stopped by the watch in his pocket.
He lived, determined not to die.

I dreamt long ago that my suburban house
Was partially submerged in water.
I could barely walk up the slippery,
Cream-colored Venetian blinds that became stairs.
In the dream, Mama spoke to me in *thlee yip*,*
Our native dialect, saying,
"*Haw luh, ai uh gung huey ghee,*"
Good, take *Gung*** home.
He, the cook at our family's restaurant,
Was a *slon doy**** who worked for us.
In the U.S., we became his family.
Heeding my Mama, I brought his gentle spirit into my house,
From that moment on, I gained a broader understanding of love.

---

* *Thlee yip* is the Cantonese fourth dialect.

** *Gung* is Cantonese thlee yip (fourth dialect) for the identity of maternal grandfather in Chinese culture. It is also a term of endearment for unrelated older men.

*** *Slon doy* are single men and married men from China who lived and worked in the U.S. without their wives and families.

I Was That Man You Saw

I was that man you saw moving around the palleted floor in the kitchen of Great China Restaurant in Oakland Chinatown. You were my constant shadow by the stovetop where I cooked — my glasses greasy, slipping down my nose as I turned on the stove. I grilled veal cutlets, pork chops, chicken-fried steak to a golden brown, not letting myself hear the hushed cries of faraway family where whispers of hope swooshed through the open window, a sight I now see in my dreams. Faintly.

I was that man you saw on our days off from Great China, walking on the streets of downtown Oakland with your *Baba* and Mama, stopping for a bite to eat at Washington Market after going to see the Lone Ranger and Hopalong Cassidy at the Fox Oakland and Paramount Theaters, temples of art deco architecture. Those television cowboys brought justice to the forlorn, saving God-fearing citizens in Hollywood films. Would they have saved us? Long-suffering waiters, cooks, dishwashers of Chinatown who seldom spoke English, who didn't even know how to ask for overtime pay.

I was that man you saw alone in my Chinatown sepia-papered room, the *slon doy fong*,* filled with musty air, the dim light dangling from a single light bulb, the one-burner stand for cooking, the tiny hallway toilet and bathtub I shared with other *slon doy*.** I was alone, but not forsaken. Because for six days of the week you, the sixth daughter, were by my side, along with your sisters and brother, your *Baba* and Mama — my *Gim Sahn**** family.

---

* *Slon doy fong* is a small bedroom in dingy apartment houses in the hearts of U.S. Chinatowns, usually rented by single and married men from China.

** *Slon doy* are single and married men from China who lived and worked in the U.S. without their wives and families.

*** *Gim Sahn* in Cantonese thlee yip (fourth dialect) literally means Gold Mountain, which is a Chinese name for the United States of America.

This poem was inspired by Ted Kooser's poem "That Was I," in *Delights and Shadows* (Port Townsend, WA: Copper Canyon Press, 2004). A previous version was published in the Winter 2016 issue of *Blue Collar Review*.

Like a Ghost

Like a ghost, you hover over me
In my far-from-Chinatown dream.
A *slon doy** and the second cook at our family's
Oakland restaurant in the 1940s to 1960s,
You smell like sugar, flour, musty wallpaper.
Your deep-socketed eyes sink into your gaunt face,
Skeletal cheeks indented by your use of opium.
Who will dip their bucket there to pull dreams upward,
Fantasies you left behind, songbirds as companions?
Do you hear the wail of your woman you wed long ago,
Before you came alone with other *slon doys*
Who immigrated to *Fah Kee Gwok*** in search of work?
Your young wife bride marooned in China,
Whose plaits you once brushed, her perfume massaging your soul,
When your bodies electrified through touch.
You float in my reverie.
Cobwebs drape through your gnarled fingers,
Your hands that once chopped onions into pearls,
No longer caressed by your woman.

---

* *Slon doy* are single and married men from China who lived and worked in the U.S. without their wives and families.

** *Fah Kee Gwok*, Land of the Flowery Flag, was one of the Cantonese thlee yip (fourth dialect) names for the U.S.

FRAGMENTS OF MY CHILDHOOD

When he sits in the tiny office
With space for one,
Baba flicks the rods
Of the wooden abacus,
An ancient calculator.
His scratched fingers are strong,
Pushing wooden beads,
Smooth to his touch,
Sounding louder than snapping fingers.
With receipts on the desk,
He calculates costs
Of a side of beef,
Sacks of potatoes, rice,
Flour, sugar,
Crinkly loaves of Kilpatrick's bread,
Cartons of cinnamon-spiced apple slices,
Leafy vegetables,
Purchased to feed
Those who walk through the
Double-glass doors of Great China,
Ai Joong Wah.*
I recall dark wooden booths,
Gold-trimmed oval mirrors,
Salmon-colored Formica counters,
Soda fountain at one end,
Refrigerator humming
At the side of the steam table,
Fragments of my childhood.

---

* Ai Joong Wah is the Cantonese thlee yip (fourth dialect) pronunciation for Great China, the name of our family's restaurant, which we ran from 1943 to 1961.

A Paper Napkin

In Oakland Chinatown long ago,
My American-born sisters and I
Became friends with Timothy, Daniel, and Bobby,
The sons of another restaurant family
Who worked next door to our restaurant
On Webster Street.
Our parents were partners once,
When they co-owned the restaurant known as Harry's Cafe.
After a falling-out, my father opened
Great China Restaurant next door.
Their broken relationship did not, however,
Interfere with our friendship with the boys.
Using a crunched-up milk carton and a wooden tennis racket,
We played baseball on Webster Street.
One time, I batted the milk carton so hard,
It broke the restaurant's neon sign.
We chased one another in games of tag,
Threw Boy Scout knives on dirt mounds
To take imaginary land from one another,
In imitation of World War II battles.
We played these games in front of our families' restaurants.
Sometimes, I sat on our stoop with Doreen Jone,
The boys' cousin who was also the daughter of Harry's Cafe's waitress.
I liked Doreen because she always
Wore blue jeans, never fluffy dresses.
One day, Daniel, the middle brother,
Plopped on the stoop of our restaurant,
Holding a paper napkin.
I cozied up to him.
"Want to learn how to fold?" he asked.
I nodded, a rapt audience of one.
As Daniel started to fold and bend,

I paid close attention.
His hands moved fast, creasing a bend there,
An angle here.
His crisp folds were mysterious.
What wonders would he unfold?
Suddenly, my attention wandered to our restaurant,
Where my job was to put napkins in the metal holder.
And, as customers reached, I watched them now
Pull several from the container I had filled.
I recall a man wiping traces of syrup
And butter stains from his mouth
After eating my mother's fluffy golden pancakes.
Suddenly, Daniel nudged me.
"Paying attention?"
I returned to the present moment and nodded.
"Here's how you make this fold," he instructed,
His hands and fingers weaving together,
Like those of a magician.
Awed, I whispered, "Finish yet?"
Daniel continued to sculpt.
Suddenly, two mounds were formed.
"There." He grinned, pushing the mounds out
In front of his teenage chest,
A paper bra.

FLYING LIKE CONFETTI

Baba, wearing his fogged, rimless glasses,
Climbs the creaky stairs of the old Victorian house
On Harrison Street in Oakland Chinatown.
He opens the heavy door to walk slowly down the long hallway.
I come running with my friends, Beverly and Willard.
"*Baba*," I call.
"*Ghee Geong Bok*,"* they say cheerfully.
We clap our hands and shout, "Lake Merritt!"
"Got your bread crumbs?" I ask.
They hold up bags bulging with leftover bread
From their Oakland Chinatown Eighth Street grocery store.
Together, we hurry outside to *Baba*'s car, a 1948 lime-green Chrysler.
He starts the motor, our laughter humming along with the engine.
Before long, we arrive at Lake Merritt.
Baba parks the car quickly
And we scurry to the edge of the shimmering lake.
When I see the green-headed mallards, I squeal,
The males with their less-sartorial mates trailing behind,
Making V-shapes in the water as they come closer.
My friends and I tear open our bags,
And toss the stale bread crumbs
Flying like confetti from the sky.
Baba watches and smiles.

---

* *Ghee Geong Bok* in Cantonese thlee yip (fourth dialect) means Uncle Ghee Geong. The second and third ideograms are my father's name. Bok means uncle.

In the Busy Kitchen

Years ago in the busy kitchen of our Chinatown restaurant,
There was a delicious floor-to-ceiling refrigerator,
With small windows the cooks opened at will.
The refrigerator was stuffed with fresh meat
And mounds of raw noodles waiting to be boiled
On the stovetop or stir-fried in the giant wok.
When the cooks or the dishwasher were not looking,
I, a nine-year-old, who helped in the kitchen,
Stole strands of raw noodles to chew on,
A sprinkle of telltale flour dusting my lips.
Racks of prime rib chilled on a refrigerator shelf,
Waiting to be roasted in the oven below the oiled grill,
So that we could put on our menu a meal of prime rib,
Costing the extravagant sum of a dollar an order.
A large gurgling pot of broth sat on a separate burner.
My job was to toss leftover bones and bits of scrap meat,
Into the bubbling pot, slow-cooking broth for the day.
In the evening when the restaurant closed, I assisted
One of the hardworking cooks to carry
The heavy pot into the walk-in refrigerator.
A scale dangled in a small room not too far away.
There *Baba* would weigh slabs of meat,
The butcher delivered almost daily.
Baba never wanted to be cheated.
So when slabs of marbled meat arrived,
He would plop the meat on the scale
To make sure that a five-pound slab really weighed five pounds.
Even though I was welcomed in the grill area of the busy kitchen,
I loved the baking section the best.
There I shadowed the second cook, who also baked.
"*Loy bong ngnoy*, come help me," he would say in *Hoisan Wa*,
The dialect of our ancestral region in China.

I clapped my hands, delighted that he asked me to help.
Then I scooped flour onto the baking table.
He grinned when flour coated my hands and face.

A previous version of this poem was published in the Autumn 2016 issue of *Blue Collar Review*.

Within the First Order

I place this within the first order of childhood memories: My *thlom gauck ngon** sister standing alone on the bejeweled front porch of Ai Joong Wah, Great China, our family's restaurant. I don't remember what part of the year she was standing on the porch — smiling, pinching her apron, lost in realms of joy. Her thin arms resting on her tiny stomach probably filled with her favorite ham and cheese sandwich, her shoulders sloping as if a rope pulled her towards gravity. Her eyes almost shut, cradling daydreams in her work at Ai Joong Wah. She was laughing. As she frolicked in the corner of the porch, I snapped her image with my Brownie box camera to nourish my memories today.

---

* *Thlom gauck ngon*, a three-corner eye, in Cantonese thlee yip (fourth dialect) means a single eyelid.

My poem is inspired by Ted Kooser's poem, "Gyroscope" in *Delights and Shadows* (Port Townsend, WA: Copper Canyon Press, 2004).

Lincoln School

I reach into the time that I was seven years old,
When I played kickball in the schoolyard,
When my sisters and I, during a break,
Snacked at the small food shack across the street from
Lincoln School, which served the Oakland Chinatown community.
The specialty?
Red-sauced spaghetti stuffed into paper cones,
Eaten with plastic forks.
We scooped thin noodles that splattered our faces,
Leaving curvy telltale lines we wiped before
Returning to school when the bell rang.
It was the time when schoolchildren chatter
In English and Cantonese floated in the hallways
Of our cavernous two-story main building
Divided by a central staircase.
At Lincoln School, I wore hand-me-down dresses
And shoes from my older sisters,
My hair plaited into a pigtail dangling down my back.
Tones from song bells floating down the school corridor
Of the other building across the schoolyard
Made me want to create my own tone poems.
In an either first- or second-grade classroom, I proudly recited
The Pledge of Allegiance with my classmates.
When we finished we pulled out handkerchiefs to blow our noses,
Because our teacher, Miss Moran, told us to do that.
I never asked her why.

We, the Outside Kids

Inside *Wah Kue** Chinese School on Saturday mornings, my friends and I snuck in hamburgers on regular white bread and knuckle-size French fries we bought at Hamburger Joe's, the Greek restaurant located at Eighth and Franklin in Oakland Chinatown. One Saturday, the greasy odors permeated quickly in the two-room school to the inside space where Wong Dook Chaw, the principal, was teaching. We, the outside kids, with silly smiles, bit into our delicious burgers and fries. We hid behind books in order to fool our unctuous teacher who had a hard time making us behave. That morning, the creaky door gradually swung open. There stood Wong Dook Chaw, with the *sah haung*, feather duster, in hand first and then he tapped it on a nearby desk. Nervously, we gulped and hurriedly stuffed our half-eaten burgers and fries into our paper-strewn desks. Wong Dook Chaw's clacking footsteps grew louder and louder. WHACK!!! One by one, our greasy hands reddened. They stung. Those burgers. Worth the pain!

---

* *Wah Kue* is Cantonese som yup (third dialect) for overseas Chinese. It literally means Chinese bridge, a term to define overseas Chinese not born in China.

The Spoon Man

The tall skinny man,
With a shiny face,
Dressed in a sport coat,
Crisp shirt, pants, dressy shoes,
A Frank Sinatra hat,
Walks into our Chinatown
Restaurant one day.
But not to drink a ten-cent cup of coffee,
Munch chewy Parker House rolls,
Or savor golden chicken-fried steak.
Clearing his throat he speaks to *Baba*,
"Can I rent a teaspoon?
I can pay.
I will return it soon."
Baba grins and reaches for a teaspoon.
After the man leaves, *Baba* instructs me,
"When he comes again,
You know what to do."
I nod.
In a few days the man returns.
This spoon transaction
Goes on for some time.
One day, I flip through the pages
Of the *Oakland Tribune*
And see a picture of a police lineup.
There, in the photo, stands the spoon man,
Next to other suspects.
The caption reads,
"Local dope dealers arrested."

BEING DELIVERED

Tomorrow I celebrate,
Seven decades and eight years of life,
Nurturing memories, I look back
To the time I turned fourteen,
A freshman at Oakland High School,
At our family's restaurant in Chinatown,
I am pouting, speaking loudly to my Mama.
"I WANT cake from Angel Kakery,
By Lake Merritt.
I don't want cake from that old-fashioned Eastern Bakery."
We go back and forth with our quarrel.
Soon, Mama gives in,
Something she would not have done
When she first came from China many years ago.
She finally understood *give and take*,
A practice in the Western world.
Elated, I run to our tiny office,
Pick up the phone and call,
Give the bakery all the details,
Then search triumphantly for Mama,
Who is carrying a plate of veal cutlets to a customer.
A few days later on Wednesday, our day off,
Mama and *Baba* cook for my fourteenth birthday dinner.
Instead of customers sitting at counter seats and in wooden booths,
My siblings, some married sisters, their husbands, and children fill the seats.
After the delicious meal, a brother-in-law asks about my cake.
Being delivered, I say, hoping my quavering voice isn't too noticeable.
After waiting a long time, one by one they leave,
My young nieces and nephews snoring on their fathers' shoulders.
When Mama and *Baba* lock the door to our empty restaurant,
My tears fall.

Som See Nai

Pink-faced *Som See Nai*,*
With a wavy marcelled hairdo,**
Dressed in navy blue.
She appeared on bustling Eighth Street
In Oakland Chinatown almost daily
To shop for her family's meals.
Her face dotted with age spots,
She wore a blue scarf to cover her neck,
While her dark midnight coat
Was always pinned with a jade brooch,
So different from my working-class Mama and other
Weary immigrant women who ran grocery stores,
Laundries, and other businesses located
In our crowded, mostly non-English-speaking neighborhood.
Som See Nai wore navy-colored American leather shoes,
Custom-made for her bound feet of a few inches.
In China, when she was a girl of no more than three,
Her feet were cracked.
Putrid blood soaked her damaged feet,
So they would, when healed, stay small,
As she wobbled from her girlhood on.
For, at a later age, when suitors looked at her,
She would be a *lotus feet**** bride,
A traditional identity for countless Chinese women
From wealthy families long ago.
In Oakland Chinatown, *Som See Nai* lived
With her family in a Victorian house not far from
Where shoppers emerged from double-parked cars,
Pausing a short distance from squawking chickens
Squished in metal cages,
Loose brownish-red feathers blanketing the sidewalks.
Som See Nai, like other Chinatown shoppers,

Usually searched for the freshest leafy green vegetables,
Stacked in wooden crates on the sidewalk.
The energetic children of the shop owners
Dashed in and out of grocery stores
And ocean-smelling fish stores.
Sometimes they almost knocked her over,
As she lifted her *lotus feet* shoes demurely,
Which purred on the pavement.

---

* *Som See Nai* literally means Mrs. Som in the Cantonese thlee yip (fourth dialect).

** Marcelled hairdo is a hairstyling technique that uses a heated curling iron to curl the hair.

*** *Lotus feet*, also known as foot binding, was the custom of applying tight binding to the feet of young girls to modify the shape of the foot.

On My Wedding Day

The cirrhosis in your liver spirals within your skeletal body,

Cheeks sunken, gold-rimmed glasses slipping easily down your nose,

Parched skin peeling like weathered bark,

White hair thinning,

Raspy voice,

As if someone rubbed sandpaper over it.

You whisper,

"I . . . will not . . . die . . . on your . . . wedding day."

I shiver, inhaling your deterioration,

Hoping your determined statement will become reality.

As the big day approaches, you willfully hang on.

I imagine you sitting tall in your wheelchair,

Pushed down the church nave beside me as the "Wedding March" plays.

On that actual day, you awake with a bright but worn-out smile.

Mama patiently dresses you in your now loose-hanging suit,

The blue one for special occasions.

You smell of medicine,

Hair neatly slicked back,

Yellowish eyes flashing,

Your grin wrapped with wrinkles.

I pin a flower on your lapel,

Its fragrance sweetening the hushed jubilation.

The photographer arrives to take pre-wedding photos.

Before I leave for the church I cling to you,

To grasp your thin body,

On my wedding day.

Acknowledgments

My thanks go to the poets whose workshops I attended. I am also grateful for the Cupertino Poet Laureate Program and the Northwest YMCA's Poetry Circle, which nurtured my writing. To my dear poet friend, Gloria Bares, I offer appreciation for many special moments of critiques over tea, coffee, lunch, and dinner. To Mara Grimes, another cherished friend, thank you for writing the postcard invitation text and for accepting RSVPs for the November 17 book launch.

I am indebted to Ralph Dranow, poet, editor, and ghostwriter; Naomi Rose, poetry book consultant; Kathy Skaggs, copy editor; and Margaret Copeland, designer/graphic artist. I applaud the preface written by Melanie Herzog,[*] Dean of the School of Arts and Sciences at Edgewood College in Madison, Wisconsin; and the afterword written by B. Stephen Carpenter II, Professor of Art Education and African American Studies and Interim Director of the School of Visual Arts, Penn State University. For the blurbs about the book, I offer my gratitude to Genny Lim, SFJazz Poet Laureate; Ann Muto, former Cupertino Poet Laureate; and Kaecey McCormick, the current Cupertino Poet Laureate. I am pleased that Edward K. Wong, my loving husband of fifty-seven years, helped on this project with his knowledgeable computer skills. He also took the photographs for this book.

Since starting my poetry career in 2013, my poems have been printed in *Blue Collar Review*; the East Bay Asian Local Development Corporation *Zine*, Oakland; and the inaugural April 2015 issue of the online journal *The Literary Nest*.

My deep appreciation goes to Diana Argabrite, Euphrat Museum Director of Arts and Schools, and to Julie Griswold, Executive Director, Northwest YMCA, for co-sponsoring the celebratory launch of my eightieth birthday art-and-poetry book, *Dreaming of Glistening Pomelos*, at the Euphrat Museum in Cupertino. As an alumnus of De Anza College's Art Department, I am coming home.

---

[*] Melanie Herzog's 2018 essay about my art in "Contemporary Citizenship, Art, and Visual Culture" has an extensive section about Oakland Chinatown.

Afterword

This potent collection of poems by Flo Oy Wong reminds readers of the many invisible lives that surround us daily. Through her detailed, intimate, and self-reflective poems of lives and untold stories, Wong offers vignettes with epic narrative arcs. Her poems are odes and confessions to people, places, objects, and memories. They honor lives and relationships with mothers, fathers, siblings, relatives, friends, and acquaintances as familiar and new, distant yet dear.

Her poems, like her visual artworks, tell stories of the human condition. They convey lessons about food, places, desires, fears, and dreams that transcend specific culture and languages. Shifting between the perspectives of narrator and subject, Flo Oy Wong's voice tells soft yet detailed accounts of work, spirituality, ancestors, heritage, culture that resides simultaneously somewhere between China and Chinatown. Through events and conversations, readers learn about her family members and the cultural structure against which they assess, define, and realize themselves. For example, the three poems that comprise *A Gim Sahn Hauck* are interwoven accounts of lives lived and defined in relationship to each other. Through her narrative voice, Flo Oy Wong shares with readers her own lost yet protected histories. While tracing specific family histories, readers also gain entry into practices, emotions, and challenges shared by many families and individuals over years and years.

Flo Oy Wong uses questions to fill in gaps, develop deeper understandings, and enhance interpersonal connections between people, places, and past events. Through this narrative device of inquiry, Flo Oy Wong deftly peers into the lives of people close to her, refining but not resolving her own place in the world and sharing generously what she knows with others.

— B. Stephen Carpenter II
Interim Director of the School of Visual Arts and
Professor of Art Education and African American Studies
Penn State University

About the Poet

Flo Oy Wong — artist, poet, educator — studied art at De Anza College in Cupertino and Foothill College in Los Altos Hills. During her art career of forty years, she received three National Endowment for the Arts awards. In 2007, she received an art award from the city of Sunnyvale. In 2013, when she turned seventy-five, she started writing poetry. *Dreaming of Glistening Pomelos* is her first book of poetry published to celebrate her eightieth birthday. Flo resides in Sunnyvale, California.

www.ingramcontent.com/pod-product-compliance
Lightning Source LLC
Chambersburg PA
CBHW061128070526
44584CB00033B/4258